table of contents